# Cook Up a Dance!
## Art, Music, and Dance Improvisation

### Kathie Goodale
### with Karl Jones
#### Photography by Kit Prendergast

Copyright © 2017 Kathie Goodale
Photographs copyright © 2017 Kit Prendergast

All rights reserved.
First Printing, 2017
ISBN 978-0-692-97710-1

Editor: Kit Prendergast
Layout & production www.laurapaulisich.com

Dedicated to

Bonnie Mathis
in gratitude
for her
encouragement and enthusiasm

"The art of teaching is the art of assisting discovery."
- Mark Van Doren

## Why a cookbook?

Cookbooks are meant to inspire and guide. They aren't meant to be read from start to finish. Some recipes don't fit the occasion, or call for ingredients we don't have. We page through a cookbook until we find the recipe that seems right. For seasoned cooks, nothing is set in stone. A yam can substitute for a potato; olive oil can replace butter. A good cook looks for inspiration and creates a dish based on particular tastes, often using what is ready at hand.

You can use this book in much the same way. Select the "recipes" that you like. Ingredients may be combined in any order.

Adapt them to your needs and preferences.

If a class doesn't appeal, skip it.

If you want to substitute or add ingredients, adjust to taste!

Above all, don't hesitate to bring your favorite artists and musicians to the table!

## Why should dancers learn about music and art?

Knowledge of other artistic disciplines is useful to a dancer. Music and movement have always been closely connected. Art enters and overlaps with dance through costuming, set design, lighting, and use of space.

The aim of this book is to explore musical and visual arts and relate them to dance. We look at ideas expressed in music and art and consider ways they can inspire movement.

In designing these classes we went to exhibitions and relied on art museums and catalogs. We drew on music of varying genres. Internet resources, old postcards, and books provided art background.

YouTube provides a wealth of musical excerpts as well as entire compositions. Most music can be quickly accessed through your favorite music application.

We selected existing works of art and music as they appealed to us, looking for connections and combinations to create "recipes" for dance improvisation. When possible we tied in to current cultural exhibitions or events.

For each recipe a visual artist was paired with a musical artist whose aesthetic was compatible. We examined shared themes. How did they intersect? Our students created dance improvisations based on commonalities.

In class, each artist and composer was introduced with a brief biography. Biographies are the salt and pepper of the recipes; use them to enhance content. In this book we have left the artists' biographies to be compiled by you, the reader, as you will be better able to select what has relevance and interest for your students.

Students were asked to look at visual art for things like color, shape, texture, content, spatial concepts, brushwork, materials, scale, symmetry and asymmetry.

Students listened to music for things like dynamic differences, tempo, rhythm, key changes, instruments, and different moods of major and minor keys.

Styles and similarities were noted. Themes emerged.

Students then discussed how these themes could relate to movement. They experimented, created dances, performed, and critiqued each other.

These experiences led to further discussion regarding possible ways to improvise in dance.

As a general introduction to improvisation, five movement concepts were introduced; all components of choreography. These concepts were referred to throughout the classes.

1) movement quality..............................sharp (staccato) or smooth (legato), strong or yielding, sustained or abbreviated

2) movement tempo..............................fast or slow

3) movement shape..............................contained, open, expanded, geometric, large, small

4) movement direction..........................forward, back, to the side, on the diagonal or in a circular pattern

5) movement level................................low and giving in to gravity, regular upright stance, high, elevated, reaching

Students were directed to move through the room exploring these five concepts.

These concepts were combined with basic dance steps: walk, run, leap, turn, slide, hop, and jump.

Choices were made as to how to enter and exit performance space: in unison, in succession, all from one side, from opposite sides, or begin and end on stage.

A phrase could be repeated with another body part, or taken up by another dancer.

Note: Children don't like to be still. Holding a shape is not dancing to them. But they learn that holding a shape creates a strong counterpoint which enhances movement.

Holding a shape can be an important aspect in the creation of a dance.

# 1

# FORMALITY AND ORNAMENTATION

**RECIPE #1**

**FORMALITY
AND ORNAMENTATION**

| | |
|---|---|
| **MUSIC:** | **FRANCOIS COUPERIN** |
| | L'Amphibie |
| | Concerts Royaux |
| | La Menetou |
| *Musical ingredients:* | ornament |
| | trill |
| | grace note |
| | theme and variation |
| **ART:** | **ROYAL CHATEAU DE VERSAILLES** |
| *Art ingredients:* | symmetry/asymmetry |
| | formality |
| | structure |
| | pattern |
| | grandeur |

Recipe for improvisation:

Introduce Couperin's biography. Play samples of music on piano, recorder, or harpsichord. Have students listen for ornament in Couperin's music. What does musical ornament sound like?

Video options:
Show videos of musical dance forms: Pavane, Gaillard, Sarabande, Gavotte, Gigue.
-or-
Show videos of Versailles gardens. Discuss fountains as ornaments to formal landscape design.

Introduce the ideas of royalty and grandeur. Discuss: what does royal, grand movement look like?

Have students create royal movement, combining formal design with ornamentation. Choose a body part and explore its decorative possibilities.

# 2
# POWER OF THE OCEAN

**RECIPE #2**

**POWER OF THE OCEAN**

| | |
|---|---|
| **MUSIC:** | **Edward Elgar**<br>Sea Pictures: Where Corals Lie<br>**Arnold Schoenberg**<br>Pierrot Lunaire<br>**Benjamin Britten**<br>Four Sea Interludes |
| *Musical ingredients:* | orchestration<br>crescendo<br>diminuendo<br>legato/staccato |
| **ART:** | **Winslow Homer**<br>Maine Coast<br>Northeaster |
| *Art ingredients:* | magnitude<br>waves<br>vertical & horizontal<br>direction<br>force |

Recipe for improvisation:

Discuss Elgar's life and listen to his musical representations of the sea. Listen to Schoenberg and Britten. Ask students to describe what they hear in the music.

Examine Homer's paintings.

How is the ocean's size and movement represented in the musical selections and in Homer's painting?

Consider the ocean's magnitude and force. Ask students to use large, expansive movements to completely fill the space. Have students use their bodies to create the immensity of waves. Explore a variety of levels, direction and force. Incorporate elements of power.

Set aside individuality, and try collaborating and working in a large group.

# 3
# IMPRESSIONISM

**RECIPE #3**

**IMPRESSIONISM**

| | |
|---|---|
| **MUSIC:** | **Claude Debussy** |
| | La Mer |
| | **Maurice Ravel** |
| | Jeux d'Eaux |
| *Musical ingredients:* | modulation |
| | *fluidity* |
| | *chromaticism* |
| **ART:** | **Claude Monet** |
| | Morning on the Seine at Giverny |
| | Water Lilies |
| | Rapids on the Petite Creuse at Fresselines |
| *Art ingredients:* | color |
| | *light* |
| | *reflection* |
| | *short, rapid brushstrokes* |
| | *spontaneity* |

Recipe for improvisation:

Discuss Debussy's biography and listen to his music. The music flows without a specific beginning or end. Melodies appear and disappear.

Introduce Monet's biography. Highlight Monet's use of gestural, abbreviated brushstrokes.

Have students create impressions of color, nature, water, and atmosphere through movement.

Avoid outlining. Avoid preconceived patterns. Avoid rigid forms.
Include spontaneity. Include flowing, indirect, gestural movement.

Move quickly, solo or in groups, pose briefly. Incorporate new directions or levels.

© Estate of Roy Lichtenstein

A scene from class:

Three boys choose a handshake as their everyday gesture. They circle the studio several times shaking hands.

"Is that it?" asks the teacher.

"Just wait," is the reply.

The teacher waits.

Soon two of the boys surround the shorter one.

The third boy begins jumping to the rhythm of a handshake.

# RECIPE #4

## EVERYDAY GESTURE

**MUSIC:** **Duke Ellington**
Happy Go Lucky Local
Isfahan
Take the 'A' Train

*Musical ingredients:*
*arrangement*
*collaboration*
*collective improvisation*
*urban sounds*

**ART:** **Roy Lichtenstein**
Artist's Studio No. 1 (Look Mickey)

*Art ingredients:*
*content*
*popular culture*
*comics*
*flat shapes*
*dialogue*
*Benday dots*

Recipe for improvisation:

Introduce Ellington's biography mixed with musical illustrations. Listen for train sounds in "Happy Go Lucky Local" and "Take the 'A' Train." How does Ellington incorporate the everyday into his music?

Listen to Ellington's updated version of Tchaikovsky's Nutcracker Suite. What is the same? What is different?

Explain that copying classics has been a long tradition for students of visual art. Compare Lichtenstein's updated *Goldfish Bowl II* painted in 1978 with Matisse's original *The Goldfish*, painted in 1910.

Discuss "updating": a contemporary approach to copying, involving experimentation.

Introduce short biography of Lichtenstein and ask students: Where do everyday objects appear in Lichtenstein's work? What are Benday dots and why does he use them?

Have a discussion about the "everyday" in students' lives and have dancers translate their everyday world into gestures. Are these gestures high or low? Forceful or gentle? Real or abstract? Fast or slow? Is there any place for dialogue?

Work individually or in groups. Combine gestures, add new ones, mix.

# 5
# AMERICAN SCENE

© 2017 Georgia O'Keeffe Museum / Artist's Rights Society (ARS), New York

**RECIPE #5**

**AMERICAN SCENE**

| | |
|---|---|
| **MUSIC:** | **Aaron Copland** |
| | Appalachian Spring |
| | Billy the Kid |
| | Rodeo |
| | I Bought Me a Cat |
| *Musical ingredients:* | *atonality vs. harmony* |
| | *folk influence* |
| **ART:** | **Georgia O'Keefe** |
| | Bella Donna |
| *Art ingredients:* | *magnification* |
| | *monumentality* |
| | *scale* |
| | *closeups* |
| | *nature* |

Recipe for improvisation:

Review highlights of Copland's biography. Explain how Copland began with atonality, which was popular with critics but not with the public. He changed his music to incorporate accessible harmonies and rhythms. Listen for folk influence in Copland's music.

Discuss O'Keefe's life. See how she used simplification and close-up views to discover the structure of flowers and bones. Discuss the (large) scale of her work, making small things appear monumental.

Students work with the unfolding of small shapes into monumental shapes.

Move from a low level to a high level.

Dance solo or in groups.

Move together or in succession, unfolding from small to large, low to high.

# 6
# STRONG STANCE IN SPACE

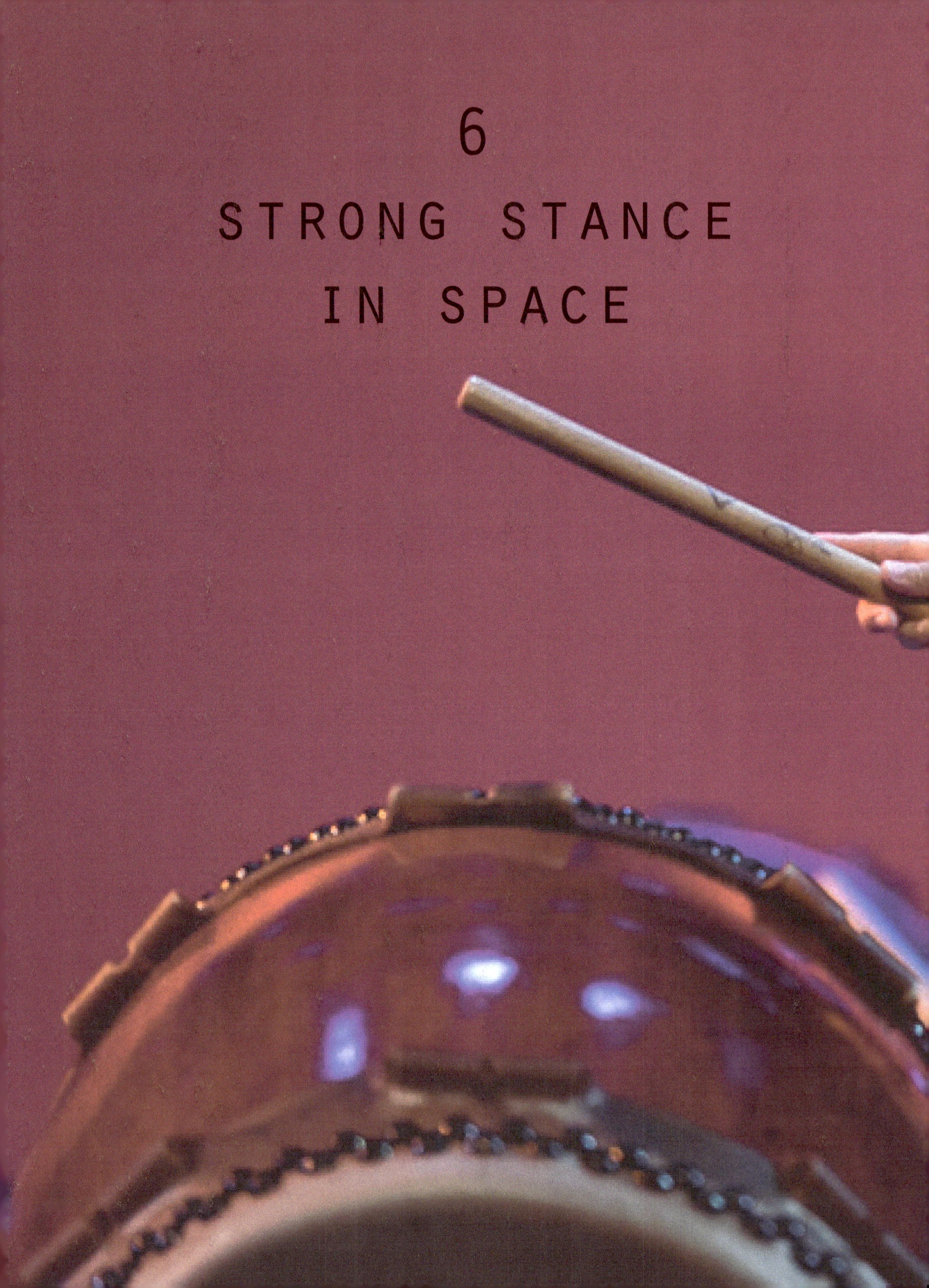

photo credit Rich Ryan

# RECIPE #6

## STRONG STANCE IN SPACE

| | |
|---|---|
| **MUSIC:** | **Taiko Drums** |
| *Musical ingredients:* | percussion<br>timbre<br>dynamics |
| **ART:** | **Katsukawa Shunshō Ga**<br>Four of the Five Actors Who Performed the Shosa 'Gonen Otoko' |
| *Art ingredients:* | portrait<br>pose<br>stability<br>deliberate movement<br>exaggeration<br>shoji screens<br>space |

Recipe for improvisation:

Listen to Taiko drums. Introduce biography of Shunshō Ga (18th c.) and examine his portraits of actors.

Have students assume the actors' poses and copy their facial expressions. Move to the rhythm of the Taiko drum as you imagine the actor would move, based on his pose and facial expression.

Experiment with different tempos and directions. Respond to the other actor-dancers.

In Japanese houses, space is changed using "shoji screens." Have some students carry large cardboard sections around the room to change the space around the other dancers.

# 7
## CHANCE DANCE

Robert Rauschenberg Trophy II (for Teeny and Marcel Duchamp), 1960 Combine: oil, charcoal, paper, fabric, printed paper, printed reproductions, necktie, sheet metal, and metal spring on seven canvases with chain, spoon, and water-filled plastic drinking glass on wood 90 x 114 x 5 inches; overall (228.6 x 289.6 x 12.7 cm) Walker Art Center, Minneapolis Gift of the T.B. Walker Foundation, 1970

BREAK → THE RULES

**RECIPE #7**

**CHANCE DANCE**

| | |
|---|---|
| **MUSIC:** | **John Cage**<br>Perilous Night<br>4'33"<br>RADIO5 |
| *Musical ingredients:* | nonstandard instruments<br>chance<br>silence |
| **ART:** | **Robert Rauschenberg**<br>Trophy II (for Teeny and Marcel Duchamp) |
| *Art ingredients:* | mixed media<br>combines<br>materials<br>found objects |

Recipe for improvisation:

Begin with biography of John Cage. Perform Cage's 4'33" in which musicians gather with their instruments and perform the three (silent) movements.

Provide dancers with 6 boomboxes, each tuned to a different radio station. Have students listen to ambient sounds in the room.

Have students randomly raise and lower the volume on their boombox. Discuss what students hear.

Continue with biographies of Duchamp and Rauschenberg. Examine found objects in their work. Look at Rauschenberg's Combines: ask students if they think chance played a role in his art?

Ask students to perform a dance guided by chance. Set major dance elements but allow chance to add variations.

Divide students into musicians (with boomboxes) and dancers and send them to separate locales to practice and prepare their dances and music.

Bring the students together. The dancers perform, not having heard the musicians. The musicians play, not having seen the dancers.

We hope that you will find success with these recipes and go on to create your own. Cook up a dance!

Thank you

To Toni Pierce, Laurel Keen, Kaitlin Bell, and the students and parents at TU Dance.

To Laura Greenwell, Lori Gleason, Preston Stockert, and the students and parents at St Paul Ballet.

To Karl Jones for having the idea of a cookbook, and for his dedication to designing and collaborating on this curriculum.

To Rick Shiomi and Jen Weir.

To Lisa First and Mako Okatake for help with permissions.

To Julia Sutter for her advice and feedback.

To Rich Ryan, the estate of Roy Lichtenstein, the Rauschenberg Foundation, and the Georgia O'Keeffe Museum in Santa Fe, for permission to include photography and artwork.

To Toni Pierce for arranging the dancers for the cover photos, and to Laurie Schneider for her expertise.

And, to Laura Paulisich for her contagious optimism and confidence.

*After dancing at Minnesota Dance Theater, Kathie Goodale went on to spend 40 years teaching modern dance, technique, and dance improvisation to children at Minnesota Dance Theater and at Ballet Arts Minnesota, where she was a co-founder. Kathie has taught dance improvisation in Japan and Russia. She has performed in Yaroslavl, Vienna, and Minneapolis, danced in "Salmon, Marshmallow, Bear and Dancer" and "Petrushka," and choreographed a Tai Chi Variation in 2014 in memory of her late husband, Robert Goodale. Kathie has performed at The Bryant Lake Bowl, The Cowles Center and The Walker Art Center Choreographic Evening in Minneapolis. She is on the Board of Link Vostok.*

―――

*Karl Jones has played piano for professional ballet dancers and ballet students for over 30 years. In the MN region, he has played primarily for Ballet Arts Minnesota, Minnesota Dance Theater, St. Paul City Ballet, and the University of MN Dance Department. Karl has also accompanied the touring companies of American Ballet Theater, the Feld Ballet, Twyla Tharp, the dance troupe of the Metropolitan Opera, and others.*

―――

www.ingramcontent.com/pod-product-compliance
Lightning Source LLC
Chambersburg PA
CBHW061818290426
44110CB00026B/2914